Contents

Photograph opposite:
All Saints' from the south
east. Richard Adams.

Quick Tour

Font The bowl is Transitional Norman, late 12th century. The base may be from a 14th century churchyard cross. The intersecting arches on the bowl are unevenly proportioned.

The Clerestory The windows above the nave arcades were put in to give more light and the roof was raised. The earlier roofline can be seen as an inverted V on the west wall of the nave.

Tower and spire Construction started in the 14th century. Completed by stages in the 15th century as money became available. The spire is a parapet or needle spire. The west door and 14th century window are contained in one large embrasure which is uncommon. The three figures are Our Lord, St Peter and St Paul.

14th century capitals This church is famous for the carving of the capitals at the top of the nave columns. Look for the Green Man; Reynard the Fox; the Pelican and the Monkey.

Consecration Cross Outside the west wall of the porch. There could be as many as 12 outside a church.

Porch and South Door The porch is mainly 13th century Early English style. The door is earlier about 1200. The stone benches were the only seating in medieval times when the porch was used for parish meetings. Note the blind arcade of arches on the walls and nail head ornamentation

e Pulpit This is
ominent so that
 Vicar can be seen
d heard.
wadays churches
e a sound system
that even a quiet
ce can be heard.
ce this pulpit had
ounding board or
er above it. You can see where it
s. Can you find from a brass plaque to
om it is dedicated?

Lectern This
is a reading
desk. The
eagle stands on
the globe.
Eagle lecterns
have been used
for centuries.
This one dates
from 1897.

Aumbry In the
Trinity Chapel. The
Blessed Sacrament
to be taken to the
sick is reserved in
it. A light hangs
nearby to show it
is present.

The Organ Installed in 1996 the organ fills
the Trinity Chapel arch. Note the Rutland
coat-of-arms which has been hand-
painted.Can you see the camera on a pillar
which the organist needs to see the west end?

Altars The sacrament of Holy
Communion is celebrated at the
altars. Three are fixed at the
east end. The fourth is in the
south transept and moved into
the nave when needed.

cina There are
 in the church
south of an altar
 where one was).
y were for
shing
mmunion vessels
edieval times.

The Chancel
The choir stalls are
here. Note the
gilded and enriched
roof, also the high
quality Victorian
woodwork of the
screens separating
Chancel from the
Chapels.

Stoup To the
right of the
Priest's door on
the outer wall of
the Sacristy.
Once contained
holy water.

Introduction

All Saints' parish church is at the heart of the historic settlement of Oakham, the county town of Rutland, and the single largest church in the county. Along with the adjacent castle – celebrated for its outstanding Romanesque great hall – and the original Tudor building housing Oakham School on the north side of the churchyard, it provides a focused ensemble for the town which has spread out on all sides from this spot. The nearby historic market place with its Butter Cross completes this picture.

All Saints' church is essentially a late 13th century and early 14th century building over the first stone church on the site of c 1200. There was a further large scale rebuilding c 1390-1410 but little thereafter was undertaken until the substantial restoration by Sir George Gilbert Scott in the mid-19th century.

Recent additions include the Mayhew Room and the narthex in the west end also the new organ located in the Trinity Chapel. There is much of interest in the church's fittings and the generous proportions of the building alone cannot fail to impress any visitor.

James Stevens Curl writing in *Country Life* (May 17,1984) comments on 'the huge Church of All Saints'...is the second most important building in Oakham. It has a noble tower and spire that dominate the town and can be seen from afar. All Saints' was an important centre of pilgrimage and is still a powerful visual presence'

The guide is divided into two sections. The first looks at the interior, exterior, fabric and fittings and the second is a brief history. A quick tour of the church is possible by using the plan on pages 6 and 7.

Photograph opposite: Nave looking west. Richard Adams.

Interior of the church

South porch and door

Visitors enter the church through the wide porch, one of the earliest surviving parts of the building, though partly restored by Scott. It is basically Early English in design c1190 reminiscent of the outstanding work of this period found elsewhere in Rutland, notably at Ketton. The porch has an outer arch of the same period, leading to four colonnades of four blind arches resting on low bench tables. The unrestored capitals are decorated with nail head motif. The second column from the south, in the east colonnade, is marble, placed there in the 19th century in the hope of encouraging subscriptions for the complete restoration of the porch. In stylistic terms the south doorway is a puzzle. It appears late Norman and therefore raises the possibility that it may be part of the first stone church, dating from around the time of the Castle.

West door and tower

The **glass doors** in the west entrance were placed there as part of the extensive changes to this area undertaken in the mid-1990s. On the south side of the tower is the **choir vestry** in which can be found a monument to Anne Burton aged 15 (1642). To the north are two rooms for parish use: the upper one is the **Mayhew Room**, named after the vicar in whose incumbency they were commissioned. The tower

area was heavily remodelled and rendered usable by Scott who reopened the arch of the tower. The inverted 'V' on the east face of the tower shows how steeply pitched was the roof of the 14th century nave. This feature was carefully retained in the 19th century restoration to indicate its original shape. The nearby **font bowl** is the oldest object in the church dating from c1180. It stood originally on eight pillars which have disappeared. Now it rests on the base of the former 14th century churchyard cross. It was in this font

Bells being taken for recasting in 1925

that **Jeffrey Hudson (1619-82)**, the celebrated Rutland Dwarf, was baptised in 1619. The tracery of the **window above the west door** is 14th century Decorated work. There is a memorial to a descendant of the poet, John Clare, **the Revd Arthur Kettle**, in the window of the office/Mayhew Room. The staircase to the bell chamber is in the south-west corner. As a result of the recent changes to the west end **a medieval-style coloured screen** was constructed separating the choir vestry and office from the nave.

The Bells were renewed after 1660 and recast in 1910 by Gillett & Johnson. There are eight altogether. Formerly, the details of the bells were as follows: 1 and 2 were cast at Taylor's Foundry, Loughborough in 1860 with 8 following in 1875. 4 and 5 were cast by Mears of London in 1858. The others were older and inscribed;

The bells were rehung with new bearings in 1979 by Eayre & Smith of Kegworth The tenor weighs 24 cwt with a diameter of 51¼ inches.

The bells are used regularly for services and special occasions although in the 1930s ringing was suspended in the belief that it was causing the tower to deteriorate. Until World War I **the curfew bell** rang from old Michaelmas Day to old Lady Day; **the gleaning bell** was rung at 8am and 6 pm during harvest. Shrove Tuesday had its **pancake bell**, whilst vestry or town meetings were summoned by **the meeting bell**. There was a **death knell** at funerals, thrice for a male and twice for a female. There was also **a Sermon bell** and one when the service was ended, known as the **pudding bell**, giving notice to housewives to hurry forward with dinner preparations. **The priest's bell** was rung just before the service as a signal for him to enter church.

Church Clock: the church has had

3 (+26) GOD SAVE THE KING T MEKINGS TOBIE NORRIS CAST ME 1677

6 IHS NAZARENUS REX:IUDEORUM FILI:DEI MISERERE:MEI 1618

7 FRANCIS CLEEVE:WILL MAIDWELL:-CHURCHWARDENS. HENRY PENN MADE ME 1723 000

a clock at least since 1684. The present clock was made by F Dent of London in 1858 as part of the general restoration. The clock face and the Westminster Chimes are based on those of 'Big Ben' on which Dent was also working at the time.

The Nave

The generous dimensions of the nave are immediately apparent to the viewer and form a major part of an interior which measures 65 ft long by 44 ft wide. The nave has **arcades** of four bays with quatrefoil piers, each with **carved capitals** in the style of leafy crockets. There are many similarities to the late Romanesque style found, most notably, in Canterbury Cathedral and in Oakham Castle. Each arcade respond is a **corbel** carved with a human face in profile on both sides of the arch. The **capitals on the north** side show the Fall of Man and the powers of evil, while those **on the south side** depict, with one exception, the theme of man's redemption.

The subjects of these capitals are:

Adam and Eve

Green Man

Chancel Arch

Tower north the expulsion of Adam and Eve from Eden
Tower south the pelican in her piety-symbol of the sacrament
1st pillar north grotesque heads and legs
1st pillar south the legend of Reynard the Fox
2nd pillar north grotesque heads and a dragon
2nd pillar south four angels facing the points of the compass
3rd pillar north the Green Man
3rd pillar south the four evangelists
Chancel north a beast with human head plays on an instrument
Chancel south Coronation of the Virgin, the Annunciation
Chancel arch damaged by the Victorian rood screen

Reynard the Fox

Coronation of the Virgin

Nave looking east

The carving of Reynard the Fox is similar to that at Tilton-on-the-Hill, 8 miles west into Leicestershire. At Oakham Reynard is seen on the north side of the capital with a goose in his jaws, followed by goslings. A man points his distaff at the fox. A fettered monkey is also depicted and two snake-like creatures intertwine, each biting the other's tail. The fox may represent the Abbot of Westminster making off with the great tithe leaving only the small tithe for the local priest (the fettered monkey). Alternatively, it could be an illustration of Chaucer's *Nun's Priest's Tale*.

Though heavily restored, **the nave roof** dates from shortly before the Reformation and consists of moulded rib and panelling in four bays. The theme of grotesque heads found in the nave corbels is continued in its bosses. The roof itself also incorporates carved angel supporters, four on each side. Double-decker galleries, the old pulpit and box pews were removed in 1857 when the **present Victorian pews** with poppy heads and other carvings were installed.

The nave aisles were added in the 13th century. The walls of the aisles were raised c 1400 enabling new windows to be inserted. The windows of the south aisle are in fully developed Perpendicular style, and there is a large frame in the north aisle filled with 15th century tracery which may have been transfered from the east end of the Chancel during rebuilding. The Decorated English west window in the south aisle dates from the 14th century. Its off-centre position shows that the aisles also had steeply sloping roofs at

this time. The carved stone lion inserted above an existing pier to support the roof beam to the east of the south doorway is also noteworthy.

Transepts

The pillars and arches are simpler than in the nave, with octagonal piers and plain capitals, probably built in the late 13th century before the nave arcade was completed. In **the south transept** these are taller than in the north. The keel shaped course of the windows in the south wall at sill level marks the upper part of the original walls in the first stone church. **The piscina** with its ancient wooden shelf is of the 13th century. The **blind arch**, now containing the Ten Commandments, dates from this period, but was raised to its present height when the building of the chapels and heightening of the church in the 15th century necessitated a simultaneous reconstruction of the transepts. Since 1980 a **moveable altar** from this transept (once known as the Holy Cross Chapel) has been used as a nave altar for family communions, two rows of pews having been removed into the Lady Chapel to make this possible. The **stained glass window** is a memorial to Charles Knowlton Morris (1905) and depicts the Rutland horseshoe emblem of the Freemason's

Catmose Lodge. The Parish Chest is located nearby.

In the **north transept** heightening was accomplished by modifying the angles of its arches while preserving their style. New windows were built in the north and east walls. The west window was retained at its original height but filled with Perpendicular tracery to match the new 15th century windows. On the west wall is a memorial to **Abraham Wright (1611-90)** Though appointed to Oakham in 1645 he did not take up his office until 1660 due to his Laudian sympathies which were not acceptable during the Commonwealth. The 'intruder' Ben King replaced him. Nearby another tablet commemorates the **Williams dynasty** as vicars of Oakham.

Chancel

The chancel was wholly remodelled by Scott when it was floored in Minton's encaustic tiles designed by Lord Alwyne Compton. **The chancel roof** is of English oak enriched over the sanctuary in the 1890s and amplified later through the donation of John Codrington.

Screens were placed in the chancel arcades and **an altar rail** of wainscot installed, later replaced by brass. **The chancel step** was brought forward 4 ft beyond its original position and was given a screen of 3ft. **An octagonal pulpit** with traceried panels was placed by the chancel arch as a memorial to Charles Knowlton Morris. **A rood screen** was erected within the arch but this was later

removed as was the sounding board over the pulpit.

The east window, rebuilt in Derbyshire marble, depicts the Ascension and was given by Mrs Doria in memory of her husband who died on 1st April 1859. It is in the Decorated style and was much criticised when installed for being the wrong period for an essentially Perpendicular church. Further limited structural alterations were undertaken in 1898 when James Forsyth's **reredos** was installed. Its architectural portions are in pink alabaster, its figures are in white. It depicts the Resurrection, angels and the four evangelists **The altar rails** of polished brass were

presented by the Earl of Lonsdale. **The High Altar** is of oak, presented in May 1944 in memory of Charles Thornton. The white Victorian altar frontal was restored and dedicated at Easter 2000. There are several more altar frontals in use.

Holy Trinity Chapel

This is on the north side of the Chancel and it dates from c 1450. It may have been financed by Westminster Abbey as a **memorial to Simon de Langham**, Cardinal and Archbishop of Canterbury (died 1370). There is **a medieval altar tomb** to an unknown occupant (probably a wealthy guildsman) with quatrefoils displaying devices which resemble sheep bells but which are more likely wool weights. **The altar** is by Sir Ninian Comper and **the window of five lights**, represents *The Adoration of the Magi* and is in memory of Col the Hon Henry Cecil Lowther MP of Barleythorpe (1790-1867), one of several prominent members of a family with Rutland connections lasting from the 1780s until

Altar frontal

15

the 1940s. There is a **15th century piscina** behind the tomb and opposite **the aumbry** by Frank Knight which was regilded and placed in this position in 1979.

The former organ was built by Messrs Brindley & Foster of Sheffield in 1872 and located in the Lady Chapel. Following extensive alterations in 1896 it lasted until the 1990s, and that despite being described as long ago as 1934 as 'ridiculously out of date and...unworthy of the church'. However, in 1937 Yates improved and electrified the organ which was moved to the Trinity Chapel. Although the console was in the Chapel the numerous pipes were some distance away filling the north west corner until removed in 1994. **The new organ**, in the arch of the Trinity Chapel, was built by Kenneth Tickell of Northampton and installed in 1995. The case is made of solid English oak and is decorated by the Rutland coat-of-arms. There is a TV on the console which allows the organist to see the west end of the nave via a camera nearby. A leaflet giving details of the organ is available from the bookstall.

The Lady Chapel

Also 15th century, probably slightly later than the Trinity Chapel. It has an arcade, a western arch, and **a fine perpendicular east window** with glass featuring *The Virgin with Jesus as a boy flanked by angels* in memory of May Clapperton who died on 9th April 1961. **The south window** of three lights depicts the *Presentation in the Temple* and is signed with the strawberry leaf emblem of Sir Ninian Comper (1913). It is in memory of John Brough Hallam and Alice Alderley, his wife, the eldest daughter of Benjamin Adam. The Chapel also has **a priest's door** outside which is a damaged **holy water stoup**. It leads to a vestry of the same period. The floor contains numerous worn memorial slabs of the 18th and 19th centuries. **The altar** is by Sir Ninian Comper and was used as the High Altar until 1944. It is a memorial to the widow of Canon Charles (vicar 1905-29). A memorial to Shirley Rowley is in south west window. There is a tablet to Harry Nicholson, organist and choirmaster for 45 years. Another tablet shows a donation for a kinetic water-powered organ in 1905. In the 1930s/40s the Lady Chapel was screened off and used as a choir vestry. The organ was located here until 1937. The model of the church was made in 1851 and shows the east end *before* restoration.

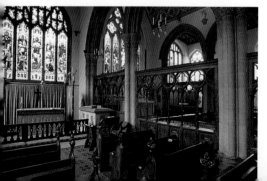

View into
Holy Trinity
Chapel

Exterior of the church

The situation of the church is significant. It is within the enclosure of what is believed to be **a Saxon burgh or fortified town**, subsequently used as the inner and outer bailey of Oakham Castle.When Westminster Abbey acquired the church this and the area to the west became known as **Deanshold**. The rest of the town, under the jurisdiction of the Lord of the Manor, was known as the **Lordshold.** This ancient division had disappeared by the end of the 19th century.

Most of the church is ashlar faced. It is all Perpendicular apart from the south porch and the 14th century Decorated spire There are large windows typical of their period, much by way of battlements and pinnacles, and Decorated friezes on the string course. **The Chancel exterior roof** was rebuilt by Scott. **The west doorway** and west window are surrounded by one giant arch. Above this level can be found three small

niches with their images still in position representing Our Lord, St Peter and St Paul. On the outside of the west wall of the south porch is **a consecration cross** dating from the 12th century church. At 162 feet high, **the tower** with its five stages, is a dominant feature of the townscape and the surrounding countryside. It contains bell openings with a distinctive rather crudely wrought battlemented parapet with string courses underneath. The **weathercock** on the spire, 'Cock Peter', is one of the oldest in England with its date of 1632, and contains a couple of bullet holes, probably from a vandal rather than damage in the Civil War. It was regilded in 1991. Roger Flore, four times Speaker of the House of Commons, lawyer and

View from church tower looking towards Oakham Castle

View of School
Chapel from
church tower

merchant, made considerable contributions to the building of the spire.

Churchyard no interments were permitted in the graveyard after 1860 when the new town cemetery was opened. The gravestones were laid flat and allowed to grass over. The Guild of St Mary was connected with a former chapel of St Mary which stood separately in the churchyard, whilst that of St Michael the Archangel had a chapel building, later **the original Old School**, now part of Oakham School. The church has a long connection with Oakham School which was founded by

Archdeacon Robert Johnson in 1584 in the churchyard, to the north of the church. For three centuries this was the only school-room. It was restored in 1723 and again in 1904 when the fine timbered roof was uncovered and a museum established there. At this time the walls were **decorated with frescoes** depicting an extract from *Morte d'Arthur* executed by Mrs Florence, sister of the headmaster at the time. In 1969 the Old School was developed as the

Shakespeare Centre but later it was restored to its original condition. To the south of the church lies Oakham School Chapel built in 1922-24 and next to it College House, formerly the Vicarage of All Saints' but now the 7th Form Study Centre of Oakham School. All these buildings together form a delightful precinct.

The war memorial is part of this scene to the south of the church and is a fine example of Sir Ninian Comper's art. It contains the names of 102 men from the parish who died on active service. Further details can be found in *Rutland and the Great War* (Manchester 1920) by former churchwarden George Phillips. To the west of the south porch there are two cypress trees grown from seed brought from the Garden of Gethsemane in 1925 by John Codrington.

History

Medieval Oakham

P re-Conquest Oakham was closely connected with the Saxon royal house in its final years. It was a developing manorial settlement centred around a wooden church. Along with the remainder of Rutland, it was granted to the monks of Westminster Abbey on the dedication of their new church to St. Peter (28 December 1065), all in honour of Queen Edith, widow of Edward the Confessor (d. 1075). This annexation to the Crown was rescinded shortly after the Conquest, the manor of the church of Oakham with its chapels alone remaining to Westminster Abbey. Thereafter links with the abbey remained important, not least because they owned tithing rights. Henry III confirmed these rights and privileges by a charter of 7 August 1252. The church still possesses a thirteenth century Latin manuscript Bible which is on permanent loan to Cambridge University Library. It may have belonged to a monastic library in the region before coming to the parish in 1599.

The first stone church was built no earlier than c.1200. It was the same width as the existing building, but extended no further east than the present chancel entrance, with what are now the transepts as its side chapels. The timber framing rested on low stone walls which reached to window sill height. The c1400 rebuilding was sponsored by Westminster Abbey, perhaps in recognition of the munificent bequest of Simon Langham, their former abbot and archbishop of Canterbury, a native of the parish of Langham, 2 miles north

The first
stone
church

of Oakham.

Oakham was not a wealthy town, though fortunes generated by the woollen trade were being made locally by the late medieval era and All Saints' was a beneficiary in two leading instances. Roger Flore was a stapler of Calais and the founder of the hospital of St John and St Anne (adjacent to the railway at the west end of the town) in 1399. He was MP for the county in 12 parliaments between 1397 and 1419, and made a significant contribution to the building of the spire. In his will he left 5 marks to the mason, a noble to be paid in 'earnest money' if the contract between them for the rebuilding of the vault of the steeple was not completed before his death. William Waryn was another merchant of the Staple, whose donations helped to build the south side of the chancel. In his will of 1499 he left a large sum for requiem masses over a 20 year period not just for the wellbeing of his soul and his family, but for 'all Christian souls in the Parish Church of Oakham' plus a gift to the municipal guilds and £5 for the high altar. There were at least four guilds in the town, all using the church as well as their own chapels and all offering money for building and repairs.

The Reformation and Civil War

The mid-Tudor period of adjustment to Protestantism was as difficult for Oakham as it was for most English parishes. In 1549, Edward VI dissolved the abbey of Westminster handing over its government to a dean and chapter and making it briefly (1550-57) the seat of a bishopric. The dean and chapter retained tithes from Oakham, but lost rights of presentation to the vicarage which, on 12 April 1549, was granted to Nicholas Ridley, Bishop of London. The parish registers begin during this turbulent era, in 1564 to be precise, a comparativly late date. The town, like the rest of Rutland, was transferred from Lincoln to the new diocese of Peterborough which, from its inauguration in 1540, was poorly endowed. It was an area in which Puritanism, 'the warmer sort of Protestantism', quickly established itself, suspicious of episcopacy, uncomfortable with the legal requirement to use the 1559 Book of Common Prayer, and wanting to continue the Church settlement of that year to a degree that was unacceptable to Elizabeth and most of her Privy Council. Puritans were holding what they called 'exercises' (meetings attended by clergy and laity for the exposition of scripture) in the town in the 1580s and it gained a reputation as a regional preaching centre. Market-day lectures (or extended sermons) attracting many of those who felt the services at the parish church were insufficiently attuned to advanced Protestant sentiments.

The result was considerable tension between Puritan clergy (of whom there were many in the parishes around Oakham) and their conformist colleagues. By the early seventeenth century, with the active encouragement of archdeacon Johnson and other members of his family, Puritan clergy from neighbouring parishes were preaching regularly at Oakham on Sunday mornings and afternoons. Puritanism in rural areas depended crucially on its gentry patrons which, in the capital of Rutland, meant the Haringtons, lords of the manor. For them the priority became godliness and scriptural obedience rather than the maintenance of the Church building. Anne, Lady Harington (widow of John, 1st Baron Harington of Exton, d. 1613) of Exton, a woman of considerable refinement and learning, presented 115 volumes of the Church Fathers in 1616 for the use of the vicar and other local clergy (housed until the 1970s in two Jacobean oak presses in the transepts). After a Faculty was granted by the Chancellor of the Peterborough diocese in April 1979, they were transferred in October 1980 to the University of Nottingham though the parochial library remains the property of All Saints' church. There is a predominance of continental titles. Some may have belonged to her son, John, 2nd Baron. He had died aged only 22 in 1614, the year the family sold the Exton estate to help reduce its considerable debts.

All Saints' church, like so many others, struggled to maintain its fabric after the Reformation as Visitation records make clear. The

John 1st baron
Harington

un dabit ȝrſyon ſalutȝ

dissolution of the guilds at the Reformation had stopped up an important source of funds to the church leaving the patron legal responsibilty for the chancel and the townsfolk for the nave. Both had other priorities, both neglected their duties. The 1605 survey gives a graphic account of the dilapidations:

'The seats on the south aisle all broken in the bottom and neither paved nor boarded. Pavements in the east and north aisles broken. The chancel and the chapel in the north aisle neither plastered not whited. Many seats in the church broken, and neither boarded nor paved. Two bell wheels broken, but being mended. The communion table unfit. The linen cloths very old. The north door in decay'.

The Visitations of 1619 and 1640 indicate further decline rather than improvement. By 1640 there were defects in the windows, roof, paving and pulpit; there was no complete prayer book in the church at the same date and a threadbare surplice had not been replaced, suggesting that Richard Tidd, vicar from 1596 to 1644, was ready to defy the archbishop and wear only a Genevan preaching gown. During the 1630s, archbishop Laud of Canterbury had struggled to overcome three generations of fabric neglect in the Church of England, but his high churchmanship and heavy-handed resort to his metropolitan authority made it difficult for his supporters to make headway anywhere in the Puritan-dominated Peterborough diocese before the outbreak of the English Civil War in 1642 destroyed Laud, abolished the Church of England, and saw his royal master Charles I executed.

But this physical decay needs to be placed in context. Elizabethan church rebuilding schemes were financed, as the nationally important example of Brooke (2 miles south of Oakham) makes clear, in the first instance by 'godly' gentry who often sought a suitable last resting place for themselves in death and a tidy house of the Lord in their lifetime; and the Puritan priority of Godly learning found expression in the foundation by Robert Johnson,

Archdeacon of Oakham (1591-1625), in Grammar Schools at Oakham and Uppingham (1584). Oakham church might have been threadbare in the late sixteenth century, but money was provided for the school which was constructed on the north side. And gifts (quite apart from the Harington library) to the church itself continued in the period down to 1640, including the Elizabthan chalice of silver gilt, 8" high with a 4" diameter bowl. It has an egg and tongue ornamentation at the foot. It bears four hall marks: an A in a pointed shield (the London date letter for 1578), a crowned leopard, a lion, and [unidentified] in a pointed shield. In 1638 the church received a chalice 'ex done Wilhelm Gibson de Barleythorp Armigeri 1638'.

The Parliamentary victory in the Civil War made episcopacy and the liturgy of the Church of England illegal, and clergy who would not accept this shift towards presbyterianism were forced out of office, like the the Rev. Abraham Wright who served only a year (1644-5), and had been instituted but not inducted, before he was obliged to give up his post. In 1645 the parliamentary side intruded Benjamin King into the living and Wright was in no position to rectify the situation until after the Restoration, when the Church of England, its liturgy and government was restored.

Eighteenth Century

For All Saints', the major change of the late seventeenth century was a change in its patron. Henry Compton, Bishop of London, by a statute of March 1696, abandoned his rights of presentation to the vicarage (in return for two advowsons in Essex) to his friend and political ally Daniel Finch, 2nd Earl of Nottingham (1647-1730), the leading Anglican layman of his day. Nottingham had recently acquired the estate and manor at Burley-on-the-Hill (as well as becoming lord of the manor of Oakham) and was consolidating his territorial influence. For the next two centuries, the link between All

Saints' and the Finchs was close, and appointments to the benefice were made with a care that reflected the active churchmanship of the family as well as their Tory politics.

Lord Nottingham had no chance to fill the living during his own lifetime, the scholarly Rev. John Warburton holding the vicarage from 1690 to 1736. Surviving reminders of this period include a flagon dating from 1725 offered by Mrs Warburton 'for the more decent communion of the blood of God our Lord and Saviour Jesus Christ within the Parish Church of Oakham in Rutland', and a plain patten of 1742 donated by Mary, daughter of John Warburton. Nottingham's son, who had additionally inherited the Finch family's older earldom of Winchilsea, instituted the Rev. John Williams to the living as Warburton's successor and thus began a remarkable dynastic grip on the parish with Richard Williams succeeding his father in 1782, and his son (of exactly the same name) becoming vicar in 1806. This run was finally broken in 1815 when a kinsman of the 5th earl of Winchilsea, the Rev. Heneage Finch, (grandson of the 3rd Earl of Aylesford), was nominated and remained in situ for half a century, the longest serving vicar of All Saints' since records began [see the memorial tablet in north transept]. Like many other parish churches in the eighteenth century, All Saints' had tiered galleries added to supplement the box pews clustered around the tall double-decker pulpit in the middle of the church. Tallow candles were fixed on to the pews for illumination. The organ (which was in a state of disrepair immediately prior to Scott's renovations) was placed in the lower of the double galleries at the west end of the church.

Church life centred on the offices of the Book of Common Prayer, with monthly celebrations of the sacrament, and an emphasis on preaching (unusually, no incumbent between 1690 and 1815 published any sermons and none of their unpublished papers is known to survive). In 1806 the churchwardens, James Preston and John Stimson, drew up inventories and recommendations for the improvement of the fabric and furnishings. It provides a fascinating insight into the life of the church in the year after Trafalgar. There were two surplices, a cloth for the holy table, bibles and prayer books. The church also contained fire-fighting equipment for the town as well as seating put aside for the county's two MPs. The sexton would march up and down during services, collaring children if they were unruly during the long services. There was also a choir and orchestral instruments for their use. The choirmen liked their ale, for at a meeting of Thursday, 7 March 1822 the parishioners assembled to hear charges of drunkenness levied against three of them. This led to a limit of £15 being ordered on the 'Singer's Feast'. Any expenses incurred above that would have to be met by the choirmen themselves. Major occasions were invariably enlivened by beer afterwards. 'Paid for ale when Mr Heneage Finch first preached, 3/-', Stimson noted in his account book. The bell ringers were another vital part of church life too receiving a guinea in 1805 for greeting Nelson's great victory at Trafalgar. Stimson grumbled that 'the Parishioners in general seem in a state of lethargy or stupefaction, as they do not support the officers as is supposed they might'. The church was unheated. In the mid-1840s, the vicar, the Rev. Heneage Finch suggested installing a suitable stove, but the parishioners preferred steam. The result was that nothing was done. The 'Stamford Mercury' reported in January 1847 that many had been deterred from attending services because of the coldness.

Scott's Restoration 1857-59

Such parish festivities were frowned on a few decades later, when All Saints' underwent a major restoration programme under the supervision of Sir George Gilbert Scott, with Messrs. Ruddle and Thompson of Peterborough making the successful tender of £4,400. Newspaper reports suggest that it was considerably overdue with the pulpit and the reading desk still covered with the black cloth with which they were shrouded on the death of William IV in 1837. By the 1850s the Tractarian emphases of the Oxford Movement were beginning to make an impact in parish life up and down the country and the work at All Saints' reflected the rediscovered priorities of liturgical ordering. Scott himself, unlike other mid-Victorian architects working in Rutland such as Butterfield, was never personally associated with the Tractarian party; on the other hand, he subscribed to the architectural orthodoxies of his day which wanted to clear away the 'clutter' of high box pews and three-decker pulpits. The changes which resulted were drastic. The main floors were retiled, as at present. All roofs, windows, arcades, tracery, piscinas and niches were restored, and the windows were reglazed. Carvings were cleaned and the whitewash was stripped; gas lighting was installed. New seating was partly financed by 'The Incorporated Society for the Building &c of Churches' which gave £200. It was conditional on allocating 280 adult seats for the poor inhabitants of the town, and 260 childrens' seats reserved for the use of the church schools. George Finch of Burley gave about £800 towards the pews, which were to be of plain deal. A specimen carved end with poppyhead, allegedly for another church, was placed against a wall in the hope he would notice it. He did so, was pleased, and donated a further £500.

Other memorable events in the second half of the century included a visit from the Prince and Princess of Wales in January 1881 when they were staying at Normanton park. They were entertained with an organ recital by Harry Nicholson, brother of Sir Sydney Nicholson and All Saints' organist for a record 45 years from 1877 to 1922 (see the tablet in the Lady Chapel). Oakham also celebrated the centenary of the Sunday School movement in 1881. Hundreds of local children gathered for a festival service as a plaque in the church recalls.

Twentieth Century

In the twentieth century, physical changes to the interior have been few. In the late 1970s a nave altar was installed to reflect the requirements of having parish communion drawn from one of the various liturgies the Church of England has deployed over the last forty years as the main Sunday service rather than choral matins; in the mid-1990s the new organ and the remodelled 'narthex' with office and meeting room also slightly changed the familiar layout. Though Oakham school ceased to use All Saints' once its own chapel was consecrated in 1924, the church has otherwise remained at the heart of civic life in the town and county, and has been well served by successive vicars, many of whom were also rural dean of Rutland. Although invariably having the assistance of two curates and at least one lay reader, the vicars of Oakham have generally had pastoral oversight of other neighbouring parishes in an arrangement which reflected the manorial descent. Thus Brooke was a chapelry of Oakham, ie not a parish in its own right, until 1884, and the large village of Langham was one down to 1913. Hambleton was added to the Oakham benefice in the 1890s and, after an interlude of parochial independence, Brooke and Langham are once more within Oakham's remit along with Egleton and Braunston. The dominant personality in the first half of the century was undoubtedly Canon James Charles (Vicar 1905-29); he was followed by two former forces' chaplains, the Rev. Albert Fraser (1929-35), and the Rev. Charles Wormald (1935-47). In their time, the services were characterised by a central churchmanship, but that gave way to a more Catholic character in the middle decades of the last century. The main reason for the change in style was the passing of the patronage from the Finch family to the Hanburys and the high church preferences of the late Colonel Hanbury. In 1947 he bestowed the living on Fr F.J. Boss, who was a former vicar of King's Sutton, an Anglo-Catholic stronghold in the south-west corner of the Peterborough diocese. His successor Canon Harry Prytherch (1951-68) had previously been vicar of St Mary's, Pimlico, a comparable church; Fr Armar Lowry-Corry (1968-78) was also on the staff there. His ministry was sadly cut short by severe illness and his replacement, Canon Alan Horsley (1978-86), opted for a simplified liturgical programme and moved the church back towards a more central churchmanship. That trend has been confirmed by the two most recent vicars, Canons Charles Mayhew and Michael Covington.

Bibliography

Basford, Kathleen, *The Green Man*, DS Brewer, Cambridge 1978

Bennett, Gary, *White Kennet 1660-1728 Bishop of Peterborough*, 1957

Britten, GE, A Pilgrim's Guide to All Saints' Oakham, Northampton nd

Cantor, Leonard, *The Historic Parish Churches of Leicestershire and Rutland* Kairos Press, Newtown Linford, 2000

Cressy, David, *Bonfires and Bells: national memory and the Protestant calendar in Elizabethan and Stuart England*, 1989

Dickinson, Gillian, *Rutland Churches Before Restoration*, Barrowden Books, London, 1983

Haddesley, Stephen, *Oakham Parish Church: A Guide*, Oakham 1972

Harvey, Barbara, *Westminster Abbey and its estates in the Middle Ages*, Oxford, 1977

Herbert, Anne L, 'Oakham Parish Library' in *Library History* no 6,1982

Horowitz, J *Daniel Finch 2nd Earl of Nottingham 1647-1730*, Cambridge 1967

Jenkins, Simon *England's Thousand Best Churches*, Penguin 2000

Longden, Revd H, *Northamptonshire and Rutland Clergy from 1500*, 16 volumes, Northamptonshire Record Society, 1938-52

Mason,Emma, 'Westminster Abbey's Rutland Churches 1066-1214' in *Rutland Record* no 5,1985

National Association of Decorative & Fine Arts Societies, *Inside Churches: a guide to church furnishings*, rev ed 1993 Capability Publishing, London

Ovens, R & Sleath, S *Time in Rutland*, Rutland Local History & Record Society, Oakham, 2002

Parkin, David, *The History of Saint John the Evangelist and of Saint Anne in Okeham*, Rutland Local History & Record Society, Occ Pub no 6, Oakham, 2000

Phillips, George (ed) *Rutland Magazine*, 5 volumes, 1903-12

Phillips, George, *Rutland and the Great War*, Manchester, 1920

Pevsner, Nikolaus, *The Buildings of England: Leicestershire & Rutland*, revised edition by Elizabeth Williamson, Harmondsworth, 1984

Rooksby, John, *The Restoration of Oakham Church 1857-58*, unpub 1995

Roskell, JL, *The Commons and their Speakers in English Parliaments 1376-1523*, 1965

Sharpling, Paul, *Stained Glass in Rutland Churches: an historical survey*, Rutland Local History & Record Society, Oakham, 1997

Sheils, WJ, *The Puritans in the diocese of Peterborough 1558-1610*, Northamptonshire Record Society, vol 30, 1979

The Story of Oakham Church, School and Castle, The British Publishing Co Ltd, Gloucester and London, 1932

Traylen, AR, *Oakham in Rutland*, Stamford, 1982

Traylen, AR, *Churches of Rutland*, Stamford, 1988

Varty, Kenneth, *Reynard the Fox: a study of the fox in medieval English art*, Leicester University Press, 1967

Victoria County History Rutland, 2 volumes and index, 1908, 1935

Waites, Bryan, *Oakham Heritage Trail*, Oakham 1993

Wright, James, *The History and Antiquities of the County of Rutland*, London, 1684 (republished 1973 by EP Publishing, Wakefield)

Most of the church records, including Registers, can be found in the Leicestershire, Leicester & Rutland Record Office, Long Street, Wigston, Leicester Tel: 0116 257 1080. Visitation Records and Bishop's Registers are at Northamptonshire Record Office, Northampton.